Copyright © 2018 by Shaiwian Mackall

All rights reserved. This book or any portion thereof may not be reproduced or used in any manner whatsoever without the express written permission of the publisher. Please send such requests to: acmpublish@gmail.com

ISBN: 978-1-7329900-1-2

Printed by: A&C Marketplace Publishing LLP in the United States of America

First Printing, 2018

FOREWORD

Minister Shaiwian Mackall has captured the art of grabbing God's Word in this busy world, squeezing out nuggets. These nuggets will inspire you for 21 days and beyond. This quick read will get your day started in the right direction and give you something to meditate on throughout the day.

~Rev. Darryl L. Godlock, Senior Pastor
Calvert County Baptist Church

Minister Shaiwian Mackall writes as one who cares deeply about the soul. She has not just read and thought about it, she is actively engaged in ministry and has discovered how real people learn to trust and obey God through their daily devotion.

~Irving L. Woolfolk, Jr., Pastor
Ebenezer Baptist Church, Supply Virginia

ACKNOWLEDGEMENT

This book is dedicated to my husband Clinton and family who has always been on my side through all of my valley moments. God used them to show me that He will never leave or forsake me.

In memory of my deceased mother, Twanna M. Wilkerson, who told me that I would go all the way! I am grateful for those words because they still echo in my spirit today!

I would like to thank Pastor Billy Stanton of Providence St. John Baptist Church, for his timely message about "Minor Adjustments!" His message encouraged me to take God at His Word. As a result of his message, I moved forward on this book, which was written four years ago.

Special thanks to my spiritual father,
Pastor Darryl L. Godlock, Calvert County Baptist Church who always encourages and believes in me. I appreciate the fatherly love and support.

A heartfelt thank you to my sister and prayer partner, Rhonda Tucker who told me one day that I should put these scriptures in a book. Well, sister, today your statement became a reality.

I appreciate my dear friend Pastor Irving Woolfolk, Jr., who told me from the beginning "Everybody is Somebody." He has encouraged and impacted my life significantly.

Thank you to everyone who reads this devotional book. I pray that these words will change your life forever. I pray that you become everything God created you to be. Rest in His bosom!

Introduction

Have you ever been in a situation that seemed to turn your world upside down? You felt like there was no hope and you would never reach the mountain top because all the odds were against you. Anxiety, depression, desperation, doubt, fear, hopelessness, and uncertainty controlled your life. You lost your focus and felt like you were crushed and slain in the bottom of the barrel. All your strength was zapped and your trust factor was depleted. Did you ever wonder how you would reach the mountain?

Even when you started to climb the mountain, the winds of life coupled with uncontrollable pollutants in the environment caused your mobility to diminish. With every stride you made, it seemed as if you were knocked down three times greater. You felt the gravity of life and you were losing your grip, strength and tenacity. As you tried to regain your momentum, it seemed as if you could not trust what you normally did in those trying situations. Instead, you resorted to what you know, but you could not get up and move towards the mountain. You wanted to just give up and throw in the towel. Your trust factor dissipated and you conceded to yourself and your ways.

In life, we find ourselves in times of doubt, fear, tragedy, and uncertainty and sometimes feel like we are losing control. We are so inundated with our circumstances and it consumes us to the point we are unbalanced and unfocused. Our focal point becomes our circumstances and we put our trust in people, places, and possessions. We forget about the Creator, who is able to do all things.

During the next 21 days, focus on the scriptures and allow them to reshape your thoughts about who you should truly trust. When we are faced with calamity, chaos, and life challenges, we place our trust in temporary things, which only lasts a moment or better said, a "quick fix". But, when we totally put our trust in God and allow Him to fight our battles and give us direction and instructions, we will no longer put faith in ourselves, people or things. Instead, we will look to God who has a permanent solution to see us through our difficult situations.

21-Day Trust Journey was birthed out of a difficult season in my life. When I felt all hope was gone, I decided to put my trust in God and His Word. In reading these scriptures during this season, it gave me faith, guidance, hope, and strength. I was able to see the attributes and character of the Almighty God, who is faithful and keeps His promises. I totally released myself and put firm belief in the reliability of God. I was not operating in my own strength, but engrossed in His grace, love and strength. I relied on God's trust, used what was inside of me and surrendered to God daily. 21 days is how long it takes to build a habit. I built a life-transformation habit of trusting God only! Honestly, this is one habit I am eternally grateful to have adopted and now it is a lifestyle of going through this journey called "life."

This 21-Day Trust Journey will invigorate and rejuvenate you to put all your trust in God and His Word. You will find yourself in surrender posture, developing an intimate relationship with your Father, and total dependence on Him.

As you begin to turn the pages, take a few moments each day to begin journaling your most intimate thoughts about your struggles. Write down ways on how you will let God into your heart and start developing a lifetime habit of trusting Him. Afterwards, write your prayer to God in the "Prayer Corner" and trust Him to answer your heartfelt prayer according to His will.

DAY 1

Psalm 20:7 ~ Some trust in chariots, and some in horses: but we will remember the name of the LORD our God.

Who do you trust? In the Bible days, people believed in horses, chariots, idols, false prophets, kings, sun, and moon. Today, we believe in cars, government, houses, man, money, people and self. We should trust in the only true and living God, the Creator and the one who gave us life. The King of Kings and Lord of Lords!!! Again, who do you trust?

PRAYER CORNER

As you have written your thoughts and reflections, write a prayer to God and trust and believe He will answer you. When He answers your prayers, please revisit your prayer request and write the date and/or how He answered your prayer.

_____
_____
_____
_____
_____
_____
_____
_____
_____
_____
_____
_____
_____
_____
_____
_____
_____
_____
_____
_____

DAY 2

Proverbs 3:5-6 ~Trust in the LORD with all your heart, And lean not on your own understanding; ⁶ In all your ways acknowledge Him, And He shall direct your paths.

How should you trust in the Lord? Trust Him with all your heart. Your trust must come from inside. Whatever is on the inside reflects on the outside. In other words, you won't look or feel concerned or worried. Even better, when you don't trust your own understanding, He will guide you. One precursor, don't forget to give him thanks! Now come on and trust the Lord because He is your everything and truly deserving of your thanks. How are you going to trust in the Lord? I am going to trust in the Lord with my whole heart, what about you?
#wholehearttrust

PRAYER CORNER

As you have written your thoughts and reflections, write a prayer to God and trust and believe He will answer you. When He answers your prayers, please revisit your prayer request and write the date and/or how He answered your prayer.

_____
_____
_____
_____
_____
_____
_____
_____
_____
_____
_____
_____
_____
_____
_____
_____
_____
_____

DAY 3

Deuteronomy 7:9 ~ Therefore know that the LORD your God, He is God, the faithful God who keeps covenant and mercy for a thousand generations with those who love Him and keep His commandments.

Why not trust God? First, He is your God! He is faithful and keeps his promises forever. He loves those who keep His commandments. The Lord will comfort, keep, protect, redeem and shield you now and forevermore! Now, I ask again, why not trust God? He is a God that will never leave or forsake you. How many times can we count people that have left us or done us wrong? I am going to trust God because He is my God. He is faithful and keeps his promises! #trustfaithfulGod

PRAYER CORNER

As you have written your thoughts and reflections, write a prayer to God and trust and believe He will answer you. When He answers your prayers, please revisit your prayer request and write the date and/or how He answered your prayer.

_____
_____
_____
_____
_____
_____
_____
_____
_____
_____
_____
_____
_____
_____
_____
_____
_____
_____

_____

DAY 4

Joshua 1:9 ~ Have I not commanded you? Be strong and of good courage; do not be afraid, nor be dismayed, for the LORD your God is with you wherever you go.

Why trust God? There are a million reasons to trust God. One, the Lord your God is with you wherever you go. Therefore, don't be afraid (fear) or dismayed (lose courage); instead be strong and of good courage. Whether you are in unemployment status, sustain hurt, pain or loss; feeling discouraged, angry or in lack, just be strong and courageous. Also, be encouraged that God is right there with you and that's assurance! Are you going to trust God? I am going to trust Him because He is always with me and you!
#Godalwayswithus

_____
_____
_____
_____
_____
_____
_____
_____
_____
_____

PRAYER CORNER

As you have written your thoughts and reflections, write a prayer to God and trust and believe He will answer you. When He answers your prayers, please revisit your prayer request and write the date and/or how He answered your prayer.

_____
_____
_____
_____
_____
_____
_____
_____
_____
_____
_____
_____
_____
_____
_____
_____
_____
_____
_____
_____

DAY 5

2 Samuel 7:28 ~ And now, O Lord GOD, You are God, and Your words are true, and You have promised this goodness to Your servant.

Why not trust God's Word? He is God and His Word is true. He has promised that you will be blessed forever. How many times have people promised you something and failed? He promised you that He will be your God and keep you in perfect peace; comfort, deliver, heal and sustain you. He is your very present help in times of trouble. You can call on Him anytime (morning, noon or night) and He will be there. I am going to trust the one and only living God! Why not trust a God that will always keep His promises and shower you with blessings today and forevermore?
#HeisGodpromisedblessings

PRAYER CORNER

As you have written your thoughts and reflections, write a prayer to God and trust and believe He will answer you. When He answers your prayers, please revisit your prayer request and write the date and/or how He answered your prayer.

_____
_____
_____
_____
_____
_____
_____
_____
_____
_____
_____
_____
_____
_____
_____
_____
_____
_____

DAY 6

Psalm 9:10 ~ And those who know Your name will put their trust in You; For You, LORD, have not forsaken those who seek You.

First, do you know God? If you know God, trust Him! God never forsakes those who seek Him. I sought the Lord and found Him. He has never failed me! Whether you are up, down, sad, angry, stressed, depressed, unemployed, lonely or hurt; take time to find God. He has a remedy for you, to give you joy, peace, love and healing for your soul. Seek and you will find Him. Trust the one who will never turn away from you! If you know God, why not trust Him? #NowtrustGOD

PRAYER CORNER

As you have written your thoughts and reflections, write a prayer to God and trust and believe He will answer you. When He answers your prayers, please revisit your prayer request and write the date and/or how He answered your prayer.

_____
_____
_____
_____
_____
_____
_____
_____
_____
_____
_____
_____
_____
_____
_____
_____
_____
_____

DAY 7

Psalm 31:14 ~ But as for me, I trust in You, O LORD; I say, "You are my God."

When plots and schemes are set to destroy you, who will you trust? Trust in the Lord, He is your God. He has you in His hand and will deliver you out of the hands of those who intended to harm you. He will hide you in the secret place, in His presence. Only God can preserve you from harm. Always trust God! He loves and cares about you in spite of your situations. Who will you trust while in harm's way? #InGodshand

PRAYER CORNER

As you have written your thoughts and reflections, write a prayer to God and trust and believe He will answer you. When He answers your prayers, please revisit your prayer request and write the date and/or how He answered your prayer.

_____
_____
_____
_____
_____
_____
_____
_____
_____
_____
_____
_____
_____
_____
_____
_____
_____
_____

DAY 8

Psalm 56:3 ~ Whenever I am afraid, I will trust in You.

In the midst of anxiety, doubt, and fear, just trust God! He knows what you are going through and He will be right there to comfort, protect and shield you. He will give you a peace that surpasses all understanding. His grace will carry you through even when it does not seem like it's going to pan out. Again, I say trust in the Lord. He has a master plan that will manifest. Say bye to anxiety, doubt and fear, because you trust a God who is greater, mighty and will never fail us!!! Will you trust or fear?
#trustGodinfear

PRAYER CORNER

As you have written your thoughts and reflections, write a prayer to God and trust and believe He will answer you. When He answers your prayers, please revisit your prayer request and write the date and/or how He answered your prayer.

_____
_____
_____
_____
_____
_____
_____
_____
_____
_____
_____
_____
_____
_____
_____
_____
_____
_____

DAY 9

*Psalm 37:3 ~ Trust in the LORD, and do good;
Dwell in the land, and feed on His faithfulness.*

In life, it seems that those who do evil or cause you so much pain seem to prosper. Don't be envious or feel hopeless because they will be destroyed. Trust in God and continue to do what's right in His sight. God will see you through and prosper you. He will even take your enemies' possessions and give them to you! Remember to trust God at all times and do good. God will reward you in due season, you will reap a harvest! Do you trust that God is faithful?
#trustGoddogood

_____
_____
_____
_____
_____
_____
_____
_____
_____
_____
_____
_____

PRAYER CORNER

As you have written your thoughts and reflections, write a prayer to God and trust and believe He will answer you. When He answers your prayers, please revisit your prayer request and write the date and/or how He answered your prayer.

_____
_____
_____
_____
_____
_____
_____
_____
_____
_____
_____
_____
_____
_____
_____
_____
_____

DAY 10

Psalm 84:12 ~ O LORD of hosts, Blessed is the man who trusts in You!

We are blessed when we trust God. He will give us His grace and glory. Also, He will shield you from all hurt, harm and danger, seen and unseen. If we continue to walk upright with Him, He will not withhold any good thing from us. Again, will you continue to trust God and continue to receive your many blessings He has ordained just for you?
#trustGodallgoodthings

PRAYER CORNER

As you have written your thoughts and reflections, write a prayer to God and trust and believe He will answer you. When He answers your prayers, please revisit your prayer request and write the date and/or how He answered your prayer.

DAY 11

Psalm 37:4-6 ~ Delight yourself also in the LORD, And He shall give you the desires of your heart. ⁵ Commit your way to the LORD, Trust also in Him, And He shall bring it to pass. ⁶ He shall bring forth your righteousness as the light, And your justice as the noonday.

Why not trust in a God that will give you the desires of your heart? Just commit your ways to Him and He will bring forth your desires. Also, delight yourself in Him. He is trustworthy and able to give you your desires! Put your trust in God who is just and righteous, and can bring all things to pass. Are you going to trust the One who gives you the desires of your heart?
#Giverofthedesiresofmyheart

PRAYER CORNER

As you have written your thoughts and reflections, write a prayer to God and trust and believe He will answer you. When He answers your prayers, please revisit your prayer request and write the date and/or how He answered your prayer.

DAY 12

Psalm 25:2 ~ O my God, I trust in You; Let me not be ashamed; Let not my enemies triumph over me.

He lifts up your soul. He will not let your enemies triumph over you nor cause you shame. Trust in a God who will show you His ways, lead and teach you His truth. I don't know who you are trusting? But, I'm trusting in God, the all wise and omnipotent one. Can you trust the God who triumphs over your enemies?
#trusttriumphpaths

PRAYER CORNER

As you have written your thoughts and reflections, write a prayer to God and trust and believe He will answer you. When He answers your prayers, please revisit your prayer request and write the date and/or how He answered your prayer.

_____
_____
_____
_____
_____
_____
_____
_____
_____
_____
_____
_____
_____
_____
_____
_____
_____

DAY 13

Day 13: Psalm 31:6 ~ I have hated those who regard useless idols; But I trust in the LORD.

I'm no longer trusting in cars, government, houses, money, people or riches. I put all my trust in GOD! God is the Creator of the heavens and earth and the giver of resources to sustain you in all your situations. When your money is gone, the government lets you down and people turn away, who will you trust? Trust in the Lord God Almighty. The one who will provide all of your needs!
#TrustGod

PRAYER CORNER

As you have written your thoughts and reflections, write a prayer to God and trust and believe He will answer you. When He answers your prayers, please revisit your prayer request and write the date and/or how He answered your prayer.

_____
_____
_____
_____
_____
_____
_____
_____
_____
_____
_____
_____
_____
_____
_____
_____
_____
_____

DAY 14

Psalm 52:8 ~ But I am like a green olive tree in the house of God; I trust in the mercy of God forever and ever.

Do you trust in the mercy of man or God? Well, definitely, I'll trust in the mercy of God at all times. God has truly never given us what we deserve! Look back over your life and see how merciful God has been to you. To say, if we were at the mercy of man, only God knows where we would be now. Put your trust in the God of mercy!!! Are you trusting in the mercy of man or God?
#trustmercifulGod

_____
_____
_____
_____
_____
_____
_____
_____
_____
_____
_____
_____
_____

PRAYER CORNER

As you have written your thoughts and reflections, write a prayer to God and trust and believe He will answer you. When He answers your prayers, please revisit your prayer request and write the date and/or how He answered your prayer.

_____
_____
_____
_____
_____
_____
_____
_____
_____
_____
_____
_____
_____
_____
_____
_____
_____

_____

DAY 15

Psalm 55:23 ~ But You, O God, shall bring them down to the pit of destruction; Bloodthirsty and deceitful men shall not live out half their days; But I will trust in You.

Trust the Lord to bring those down who cause you agony, distress and pain. God will not let them carry out their schemes and plots. In fact, He will cause their days to be shortened. How will you trust in God who will sustain you and not let you be moved or overtaken?
#triumphantGod

PRAYER CORNER

As you have written your thoughts and reflections, write a prayer to God and trust and believe He will answer you. When He answers your prayers, please revisit your prayer request and write the date and/or how He answered your prayer.

_____
_____
_____
_____
_____
_____
_____
_____
_____
_____
_____
_____
_____
_____
_____
_____
_____

DAY 16

Psalm 56:3-4 ~ Whenever I am afraid, I will trust in You. ⁴ In God (I will praise His word), In God I have put my trust; I will not fear. What can flesh do to me?

When you are afraid and people appear to be triumphing over you; put your trust in God. When people spread lies, attempt to hold you back and gang up against you, just put your trust and faith in the Lord God Almighty. He will shield and protect you. In fact, there is nothing man can do to you! How will you prevent the fear-factor from preceding God's trust?
#Godprevailsoverman

PRAYER CORNER

As you have written your thoughts and reflections, write a prayer to God and trust and believe He will answer you. When He answers your prayers, please revisit your prayer request and write the date and/or how He answered your prayer.

_____
_____
_____
_____
_____
_____
_____
_____
_____
_____
_____
_____
_____
_____
_____
_____
_____
_____

DAY 17

Psalm 62:8 ~ Trust in Him at all times, you people; Pour out your heart before Him; God is a refuge for us. Selah

God is your refuge and strength. You can put your trust in Him at all times. He hears your humble cry and will give you the desires of your heart! Will you trust God enough to pour out your heart to Him?
#trustGodwithyourheart

PRAYER CORNER

As you have written your thoughts and reflections, write a prayer to God and trust and believe He will answer you. When He answers your prayers, please revisit your prayer request and write the date and/or how He answered your prayer.

_____
_____
_____
_____
_____
_____
_____
_____
_____
_____
_____
_____
_____
_____
_____
_____
_____

DAY 18

Psalm 125:1 ~ Those who trust in the LORD are like Mount Zion, Which cannot be moved, but abides forever.

Trust in the Lord because you will be immovable in spite of what you are facing. The winds and storms will come, but like a mountain, you will not be moved. Continue to abide in Him forever and He will be with you during each situation. How will you be kept from being movable? #immovablewithGod

PRAYER CORNER

As you have written your thoughts and reflections, write a prayer to God and trust and believe He will answer you. When He answers your prayers, please revisit your prayer request and write the date and/or how He answered your prayer.

DAY 19

Psalm 91:2 ~ I will say of the LORD, "He is my refuge and my fortress; My God, in Him I will trust."

God is your refuge (shelter) and fortress (stronghold)! He will deliver you from the hand of your enemies and heal you from sickness. He will cover and shield you from all danger, harm and hurt. Trust in God, who is your shield and protection! Why not trust a God who is your refuge (shelter) and fortress (stronghold)?
#Godofshelter

PRAYER CORNER

As you have written your thoughts and reflections, write a prayer to God and trust and believe He will answer you. When He answers your prayers, please revisit your prayer request and write the date and/or how He answered your prayer.

_____
_____
_____
_____
_____
_____
_____
_____
_____
_____
_____
_____
_____
_____
_____
_____
_____
_____

DAY 20

Psalm 115:8-11~ Those who make them are like them; So is everyone who trusts in them. ⁹ O Israel, trust in the LORD; He is their help and their shield. ¹⁰ O house of Aaron, trust in the LORD; He is their help and their shield. ¹¹ You who fear the LORD, trust in the LORD; He is their help and their shield.

Do not put your trust in man. Always put your trust in the Lord. He is your help and shield. No man can help or shield you from harm and danger like the Lord God. Trust in a God who is your very present help. He will shield you from life dangers (seen and unseen). Who are you putting your trust in?
#trustGodyourhelpandshield

_____
_____
_____
_____
_____
_____
_____
_____
_____
_____

PRAYER CORNER

As you have written your thoughts and reflections, write a prayer to God and trust and believe He will answer you. When He answers your prayers, please revisit your prayer request and write the date and/or how He answered your prayer.

_____
_____
_____
_____
_____
_____
_____
_____
_____
_____
_____
_____
_____
_____
_____
_____
_____
_____

_____

DAY 21

Psalm 118:8-9 ~ It is better to trust in the LORD than to put confidence in man. ⁹ It is better to trust in the LORD than to put confidence in princes.

Well, it is better to trust in the Lord than putting your confidence in man and princes (rulers). When man fails, you can always depend on the Lord God to see you through in spite of your situation. The Lord is your strength, song and salvation! From this day forth, will you trust the Lord, man or princes (rulers)?
#trustGod

PRAYER CORNER

As you have written your thoughts and reflections, write a prayer to God and trust and believe He will answer you. When He answers your prayers, please revisit your prayer request and write the date and/or how He answered your prayer.

_____
_____
_____
_____
_____
_____
_____
_____
_____
_____
_____
_____
_____
_____
_____
_____
_____
_____

FINAL THOUGHTS

I pray that you have relished in the presence of God and let His Word permeate into your heart and mind. You can trust God, who is a promise keeper, a provider, faithful, way maker, and trustworthy. You don't have to rely on yourself or your own strength, but total dependence on Abba Father. He will continue to lead, guide and navigate you on this journey. You have a new lifestyle of resting and trusting in God your Father!

ABOUT THE AUTHOR

Minister Shaiwian is a member of Calvert County Baptist Church (CCBC) under the leadership of Pastor Darryl L. Godlock where she serves as Director of the Christian Education Department. As Director, Minister Shaiwian has instituted CCBC's Bible Institute (BI). She exercises her gifts by teaching Growth Group classes on Sunday mornings and classes at CCBC's BI.

Minister Shaiwian holds a Master's degree in Biblical Studies from Lancaster Bible College with double honors. She has a Bachelor's degree in Accounting and Business Administration from the University of Maryland.

Minister Shaiwian loves God and His people. She strives to teach others about Jesus Christ so they can become everything that God has ordained for their lives. Minister Shaiwian is passionate about helping God's people and sharing the gospel of Jesus Christ throughout the world. To fulfill her passion, Minister Shaiwian has taken mission trips, both domestically (New Orleans in support of Hurricane Katrina) and internationally (Jamaica, Nicaragua, South Africa, West Africa, Burkina Faso and Ghana), and Ukraine.

Minister Shaiwian firmly believes that through all of your agony, distress, pain, rejection and storms of life, God still loves you and you are a prime candidate to edify the body of Christ. Now, let God use you!

Shaiwian Mackall was born and raised in Calvert County, Maryland and married to Clinton. She is a devoted wife and mother. She is embarking on the new journey as an author.

www.ingramcontent.com/pod-product-compliance
Lightning Source LLC
Chambersburg PA
CBHW071800040426
42446CB00012B/2641